Skilled Customer Service

Service

JACOBIA ROBINSON

ABOUT THE AUTHOR

JACOBIA ROBINSON HAS WORKED FOR A
FORTUNE 500 COMPANY FOR OVER A DECADE.
SHE WROTE THIS BOOK TO BE ABLE TO
PROVIDE INDIVIDUALS WITH AN ARRAY OF
SKILLED CUSTOMER SERVICE LESSONS TO
PLACE AN EMPHASIS ON THE IMPORTANCE OF
A POSITIVE ATTITUDE, EFFECTIVE
COMMUNICATION SKILLS AND POSSESSING A
LIKEABLE PERSONALITY. HAVING SKILLED
KNOWLEDGE WILL HAVE CUSTOMERS
RETURNING AND TRUSTING YOUR QUALITY
SERVICE FOR YEARS TO COME.

CONTENTS

Chapter One

Having A Positive Attitude

Attitude is everything. It shapes the reality of your work, home and business. It determines the altitude of your life. Attitude has a significant impact on your relationships and everyone that is around you. It determines your level of success and is often a product of past experiences and events. Your attitude is the fundamental ingredient in every significant aspect of your life that requires interaction with another individual.

The reason for positive attitude in customer service is that such an attitude spreads and has a profound positive effect on people. Customers expect high standards of service and top-class experiences with a company –

every time and through every touchpoint. Your attitude reflects the brand and reputation of every organization, business, church or leader that you represent. Your attitude can destroy or construct. Your attitude can wound or heal. Your attitude is your biggest propeller or hindrance. Your attitude determines the dynamics of your life, goals and careers. No one likes a negative person. A bad attitude is like a foul odor in the air. It lingers and causes everyone to become uncomfortable.

Working for a Fortune 500 company for over this past decade has helped me to retain the knowledge needed to effectively communicate the significance of a dynamic attitude. As a business owner and host of an array of workshops, I wanted to empower women and men of all ages with a simple technique to getting ahead in life: Keeping a positive attitude. Having a positive attitude will attract diverse customers and will open doors that pure talent cannot open alone. I remember when my good friend started her business. She received a major contract because of her attitude and how she handled that client. As I worked for her, I was able to witness firsthand the doors that opened for her due to that admirable attribute. Her attitude was the foundation to the future she didn't even know that had already been prepared for her. To this very day, she is still in business because having a good attitude keeps your doors open longer than any competitor that may be offering an identical service. People don't know you care until you show you care and you show that you care by the way you handle those you interact with on a daily basis.

Your attitude has a profound and lasting effect on the customer's experience of a company. Given that customer service as a role is demanding, annoyances and irritation are part of the everyday operations for the service staff, and it becomes even more imperative to maintain a positive attitude while dealing with customers.

A positive attitude will allow you to see things from a customer's retention point of view and to keep customers interested and engaged while ensuring they have positive experiences each time. Vibrant and thriving businesses are filled with positive associates and managers. People love to be handled with care. A positive attitude in customer service means happy customers, which in turn means success for the company. Customers remember when they are treated well but may not talk about it. However, if they were not treated well, they would be very likely to spread the negativity through verbal or posted reviews on social media about their poor experiences. Negative attitude tarnishes reputation and hinders opportunity. What type of attitude do have?

Chapter Two

Following Up with Customers

There is power in follow-up. Customer service follow ups have the potential to influence a customer's overall experience with your company, and even affect their outlook on your business practices when giving reviews, either online or in-person. Many make the mistake of just taking a customer's money and never reaching back out to them with a thank you, promotion or simple appreciation email. It only takes a matter of seconds to show you care and a matter of minutes to gain a client for life.

Good customer service is much more than being polite, a friendly smile or resolving customer complaints in a timely fashion. In order to truly deliver exceptional customer service, customers must see that you care more than just about the sale or next commission bonus—which is why a follow up call is important and can make all the difference to the customer.

Great customer service extends to customers even after a sale is made. It builds a long-lasting relationship with your buyer. Following up impacts your business in three significant areas: repeat business, feedback and beating the competition. Repeat business helps keep you in business. If your customers feel like forgotten about after your sold them something, they may be less likely to buy from you again in the future. The customer might feel manipulated because it seems like you were just trying to make a quick and easy sale. If you let your customers know you care about them, they're more likely to feel a connection to your company and will purchase from you again.

By following up with customers, you significantly increase your overall chances of improving your overall customer feedback. A good experience evokes current customers to tell others about your company. Referral and word-of-mouth advertising is very powerful; if someone really loves your company and how you handled their sale, they will spread the word to a friend or family member looking for the same services. That's free advertising. People, especially relatives and friends, are more likely to trust recommendations from people they already know. A strong rapport with clients equates to a strong repeat sales base with clients.

And most importantly, better customer service help you beat out your competition. People don't know you care until you show you care.

If you're concerned about your competition, work on making each sale a good experience for your buyers. Don't give them a reason to look somewhere else. If you take the time to connect with your customers, it improves the overall reputation of your company. People spend with those they can depend on. Consistent communication is a necessity. It equates to consistent revenue.

Letting customers know what's going on will resolve a lot of issues. Simply put, people want to know what's going on especially if they've spent their money with you. Nothing makes someone more suspicious of a salesperson than an individual that takes their money and no additional follow-up is given. A well-informed customer is a happy customer. One of the most overlooked qualities of good customer service is the necessity of keeping your customer informed on every step of the process. People always want to know what's going on whether it be a simple email, automated text or short phone call. Customers want to be in the loop. Often times in the sales industry, we make the honest mistake of telling the customer only as much as is necessary, so that the agent is able to maintain control of the interaction, but a customer who feels completely out of control will eventually become an unhappy, dissatisfied or even complaining customer. Information is the key to easing a customer's mind, even if the information may not exactly be what he or she wanted to hear.

An informed customer is more likely to be a repeat customer when their issues were handled in a timely matter. When your customer is looking to have an issue resolved, how you handle their issue is the beginning of building their trust. Following up establishes a strong foundation and builds a lasting relationship. Why should this customer still believe in your company and return as a repeat buyer? Why should this customer suggest your company to their friends and family? What sets you apart from the competitors that offer the same services as your company? What makes a customer remember you after the transaction is completed? A good answer to these questions is to provide follow-up after a sale.

Chapter Three

Being Non-Judgmental

There's a an old saying that you should never judge a book by its cover. Now, in business, we should say to never judge a customer by their garments. Some of the world's wealthiest individuals may enter your business in flip flops, t-shirt and slightly uncombed hair. We should never assume that just because a customer is dressed a certain way that they could not afford to purchase an item that you have for sale. I recall reading an article about a sales associate that prejudged a billionaire. She followed her around the store because she did not look like she could afford to purchase anything. The woman complained and when her identity was revealed that sales associate was in utter disbelief.

Judgment certainly has its place. But judgmental communication is typically more harmful than beneficial when it comes to the business or the workplace, especially as it relates to customer service and sales. It can quickly put people on edge and make a person feel insulted or misunderstood. Judgment can cause people to become defensive. Judgement, in some cases, can also lead to lawsuits.

Your body language and word choices often reveal your true thoughts. Almost every manager or salesperson that's been in the business for a while can share a similar story to where someone – perhaps even themselves – prejudged a customer and lost a sale. Perhaps that sale was lost to another salesperson at the business, or perhaps the company lost the sale altogether. But it has happened and continues. The truth is you don't know how much a person might be ready to spend. Focus on building relationships with your customers rather than prequalifying them, and you never know what might blossom.

When you quit judging people, the relationship is untainted, and a better customer experience is afforded to everyone. Everybody deserves a fair chance at for a quality service. Even if they can't purchase your product right then or need more time to reach a decision, they will remember you when they are ready to move forward with the purchase.

With all my years' experience in business and customer service, I have come to learn that being prejudice in business is costly. Discounting a prospective customer or making decisions about their ability to make a purchase based on the way they look versus who they are, can be a very expensive mistake. Prejudging said simply, is all about you. Here, you are relying on your faulty and costly assumptions, thoughts and beliefs to determine their needs and whether this prospect will potentially buy from you. When you pre-judge someone you're making assumptions about them before you ask any questions or uncover any facts.

Chapter Four

Keeping Customers Updated with New Services

When you have a new service, keep your customers updated. People can't spend money where they do not know to spend it. You must communicate with the customers that you are looking to attract and the one's that you want to continue to come back. You must stay in the face of customers. People cannot buy what they do not know what you offer.

Taking repeat business for granted is an easy yet costly mistake in business. Just because customers leave you a positive review doesn't mean they'll return to make another purchase from you. It takes effort to earn their business over and over because competitors are always offering something at a lower price. People spend with who they see because who they continuously see is who they will remember.

While businesses often direct their attention on attracting new clients, strengthening and maintaining their relationship with existing customers is equally, or perhaps even more important.

Returning customers are the heartbeat of most businesses. An informed customer becomes an ambassador for your organization because a loyal customer is not only paying for your products and services, but they are telling others about you too.

After the sale, business owners must devote resources to continuously building the relationship instead of merely setting their sights on the next transaction. Sending clients, a special incentive, and regular communication such as email newsletters, will keep them coming back. New products create new streams of revenue.

Effectively communicating what you offer keeps the experience fresh and relevant. You must give your customers a reason to shop with you again. You can promote directly from your website within integrated mailing lists or even add notices on checkout pages of new promotions.

To stay relevant and keep your best customers happy, it's very important to continuously optimize and update your customer retention strategies. Here are a few strategies you can use:

- You can post about your new product or service to Google or you can even upload photos of the new product or service to your profile on Google Places.

- Offer your customers an exclusive product preview. This may be in the form of a private, pre-launch party, an online preview, or a special invitation or coupon to test out your newest service. Exclusive offers and previews contribute to exclusive streams of revenue.

- Contests, promotional giveaways and raffles are a very popular ways to keep customers informed especially on social media. These online promotions help to get more direct traffic, put your business in front of new customers, and for a fun way to connect with fans.

There are so many things that are available to keep your customers in the loop. Promote or boost an ad on Facebook, hang up a promotional giveaway sign outside of your business, offer an upgrade or trade. Whatever you do, just make sure you are doing something to draw attraction. Some effort is better than no effort and your business will not grow as you expected if you do not let customers know what you're offering and how they can obtain it.

Chapter Five

Believing in Yourself

If no one believes in you, you must believe in you and your product. The vision will not work without it. Self-confidence is major. It shapes every transaction and business encounter. It can make or break a deal. You must believe in yourself to be able to know your worth and the value that your product or services bring to the table.

Believing in yourself is an admirable attribute that will eventually make others believe in what you're selling. No one wants to make a purchase from someone that is clueless, unable to answer their questions or lacks the ability to be able to convey why they need your services.

Secondly, believing in yourself is a form of intrinsic motivation. Failure is indefinitely a part of the journey to greatness in business. Many are rejected and then eventually respected. What's even sadder is that many won't believe in what you say until they see what you said. The most successful individuals such as Tyler Perry or Steven jobs would tell you that they were only able to keep going and achieve success because of the level of belief in themselves despite the enormous amount of failures they had experienced for years leading up to their big breakthroughs. Their belief is what created a vision so big that they didn't care how many times they failed at something. They were eventually going to get to where they wanted to go. And guess what, they did! As a business owner or aspiring entrepreneur, you will experience a loss or setback at some point in your journey. Those experiences are what strengthen you along the way. That's not to be negative or discourage you, that's just a part of life. But when it does happen, and when your belief is strong, no failure or setback will have the power to completely wipe you out. You will use it to motivate you to be successful even more.

You must believe, encourage and motivate yourself in business and in life. You must be your own hype man and cheerleader. Be the energy that you want to attract. Thinking positive, empowering thoughts is one thing, but talking to yourself like a winner retrains your thought process. In business, you must own the stage and know that you're unique even if others offer the same service as you. Even if they try replicate what you offer, they can't replicate the vision that God gave you. Because where there is vision, He provides provision. But you must believe that success is for you.

Look at life from this perspective. If you do not believe in yourself, there is no way you can expect anyone else to believe in you and your products or services. If you are an employee, you can't expect your boss to fully believe in you if you don't even believe in yourself and show them what you are capable of especially when you want to get a raise or a promotion. If you are an entrepreneur, you can't expect an investor to believe in your ideas if you don't even believe in your ideas. How you think of yourself and your business is how others will think of you and your business. Believe in you and others will eventually too.

Chapter Xix

First Impression

First impressions can make or break a business and a positive experience can create long-lasting business relationships. Every day is a new first impression with someone that can possibly change the face of your business. The way in which you carry yourself and how you venture out in public, how you communicate with church members, colleagues and clients, and the ways you publicize yourself are all first impressions.

You never who is watching you nor are you aware the impact that you made when treated them with compassion and respect. Making a good first impression is particularly important when it comes to meeting customers, pitching to potential clients or during interviews. These are the key points at which people will meet you and begin to form an impression of you and the services you're offering. If your attitude is jacked up, hair is uncombed and your clothing is wrinkled, they will form a bad impression of you based on what you could have prevented. If what you wear, how you treat people and how you carry yourself is daily advertising of your business and brand, then what are you showing your potential investors or customers? Your customers expect your presentation to align with your posture, personality and character. What they see is who they assume you will be!

When it comes to making a good first impression, you must take the time to perfect a look. You must be sure of the image or message that you want to project and this will depend upon the market in which you circulate. If you're in fitness, then look fit, dress fit and be fit. If you're in business, then you should look and carry yourself like a business professional. If you're a web or graphics designer, you can't have a horrible personal website and clipart fliers and expect someone to believe that you are able to perfect their vision. People will not believe what you say until they see what you portray in and outside of your brick and mortar. Making a good first impression is vital and can be the difference between impressing clients and winning contracts and being left out on the sidelines wondering why no supports your brand or buys your products. Ask yourself? Would you buy from you based on how you interact with people or how you look? If the answer is no, change the impression you give off and you'll change the dynamic of your business.

Bad first impressions are costly and crucial. Giving a bad first impression can lose you the confidence of prospective investors, sponsors, customers and clients, and even cost you potential sales. How much have you lost based on lack or preparation of presentation? What are you willing to change to reshape the perspective that you have created in others of your brand? How bad do you want to be successful? Change the first impression that you set with others and you'll change the dynamics of your life.

Key Points to Remember

- Always greet your customers.

- Treat all your customers as if they are spending a million dollars with you. Remember, the janitor deserves the same level of respect as the CEO.

- Don't overwhelm customers with personal problems. Your issue is not their issue.

- Don't allow one bad experience with a customer to make you feel like a failure.

- Move forward with confidence in knowing that you can and will be successful with the right connections, resources and mindset.

- Your gift will get you in the room, but your character will keep you there.

- Confidence and integrity are vital ingredients to success in business.

- First impressions make the difference!

- People will not believe what you say until they see what you said.

- How you view your business or products is how others will view your business and products.

A Moment of Self-Reflection

When you know better, you do better. What are some areas that you have discovered that you can improve upon? Self-confidence? Communication? First impressions? Judging people? How can you contribute to the improvement of your sales process or customer service experience with your business? Use the following journal pages to acknowledge how you have contributed to the success or lack of success for your business. Then write out a plan of action for your future.

_____

_____

_____

_____

_____

_____

_____

_____

_____

_____

_____

_____

_____

_____

_____

_____

_____

_____

_____

_____

_____

_____

_____

_____

_____

_____

_____

_____

_____

_____

_____

_____

_____

_____

_____

_____

_____

_____

_____

_____

_____

_____

_____

_____

_____

_____

_____

_____

_____

_____

_____

_____

_____

_____

_____

_____

_____

_____

_____

_____

_____

_____

_____

_____

_____

_____

Jacobia Robinson

_____

_____

_____

_____

_____

_____

_____

_____

_____

_____

_____

_____

_____

_____

_____

_____

_____

_____

_____

_____

_____

_____

_____

_____

_____

_____

_____

_____

_____

_____

_____

_____

_____

_____

_____

_____

_____

_____

_____

_____

_____

_____

_____

_____

_____

_____

_____

_____

_____

_____

_____

_____

_____

_____

_____

_____

_____

_____

_____

_____

_____

_____

_____

_____

_____

_____

_____

_____

_____

_____

_____

_____

_____

_____

_____

Jacobia Robinson

_____

_____

_____

_____

_____

_____

_____

_____

_____

_____

_____

_____

_____

_____

_____

_____

_____

_____

_____

_____

_____

_____

_____

_____

_____

_____

_____

_____

_____

_____

_____

_____

_____

_____

_____

_____

_____

_____

_____

_____

_____

_____

_____

_____

_____

_____

_____

_____

_____

_____

_____

_____

_____

_____

_____

_____

_____

_____

_____

_____

_____

_____

_____

_____

_____

_____

_____

_____

_____

_____

_____

_____

_____

_____

_____

_____

_____

_____

_____

_____

_____

_____

_____

_____

_____

_____

_____

_____

_____

_____

_____

_____

_____

_____

_____

_____

_____

_____

Jacobia Robinson

_____

_____

_____

_____

_____

_____

_____

_____

_____

_____

_____

_____

_____

_____

_____

_____

_____

_____

_____

_____

_____

_____

_____

_____

_____

_____

_____

_____

_____

_____

_____

_____

_____

_____

_____

_____

_____

_____